# THE ECHOING GREEN

Gillian —
all good wishes —
hope you'll enjoy these
Shropshire poems —
Gladys Mary
16/6/09

Also by Gladys Mary Coles

# THE ECHOING GREEN

## Gladys Mary Coles

*Gladys Mary Coles*

**FLAMBARD**

First published in England in 2001 by Flambard Press
Stable Cottage, East Fourstones, Hexham NE47 5DX

Typeset by Harry Novak
Cover design by Gainford Design Associates
Author photograph by Fred Edwards
Printed in England by Cromwell Press, Trowbridge, Wiltshire

The image used on the front cover is taken
from a photograph by Gladys Mary Coles of
Spring Coppice, Mary Webb's 'Little Wood', Lyth Hill.

A CIP catalogue record for this book
is available from the British Library.

ISBN 1 873226 48 9

Flambard Press wishes to thank Northern Arts
for its financial support.

Website: www.flambardpress.co.uk

# CONTENTS

**Kingdom of Sphagnum**

**Histories**

**The Land Within**

# Kingdom of Sphagnum

Fenn's, Whixall, Bettisfield, Wem and Cadney Mosses,
a wilderness between Wales and England

*'No words that I know of will say what mosses are.'*
John Ruskin

# AUTHOR'S NOTE

'Kingdom of Sphagnum' is a sequence of poems about an histori-
cally and ecologically important complex of wilderness straddling
the border between Wales and England. This evocative landscape
of some 2,500 acres is situated where a corner of Wrexham County
(formerly Clwyd) meets north-west Shropshire.

Fenn's, Whixall, Bettisfield, Wem and Cadney Mosses form an
enormous expanse of peat bog, the third largest lowland raised
mire in Britain, dating back more than 10,000 years to the post-
glacial period. It is a unique habitat of a wide range of plants and
animals, many of which are rare species.

The Mosses have survived 400 years of peat extraction, includ-
ing commercial cutting and, in 1989–90, an intensive mechanised
commercial operation. A campaign to save the Mosses from des-
truction by peat exploitation was successful in 1990. They are now
under the joint stewardship of the Countryside Council for Wales
and English Nature, for conservation and management as a National
Nature Reserve. The Mosses are a Site of Special Scientific Interest
and a Wetland of International Importance.

The sequence of poems moves in a gyre, from present time into
the past, and then back again to the present day. It begins with two
long poems on my exploration of the Mosses, a personal response
to this border wilderness, a physical and spiritual journey. It then
moves into past decades, imaginatively exploring aspects of the lives
of peat-cutters and their families, men and women of the locality
who, generation after generation, drew a living from the Mosses.
Some of the poems are in their imagined voices and personae.

The sequence concludes with a return to today and my personal
exploration in 'Dragonfly Weather', a celebration of the National
Nature Reserve.

# KINGDOM OF SPHAGNUM

## The Boundary

Bark border of the peat prairie,
forest, where birds have freehold,
lichen has licence.

Fox-haven, weasel-covert,
home of vole and leaf beetle,
of badger, hare, lizard.

Here, logs piled in pyramids
are threshold guardians, warn
of selective felling.

Maps show other borders:
radial band of road,
the canal's slow coil,
a railway's relentless parallels.

Fixed lines on the map
tell lies about territory:
Wales exactly here, England there.
False frontiers, invaded by winds,
by seeds, spores, germs.
On the winds the whisper of languages
blown either way, reversing directions.

No line fractures the bog –
Fenn's, Whixall, Oaf's Orchard…
the given names for one being.
No margins in the mosses,
kingdom of sphagnum
where space and time interweave.
Border here is where
air meets earth, light meets landscape.

This blue line on the map
depicts water: a solid straightness
of canal; there a wriggle of river,
a filament of stream.

Yet all here is liquid,
names labelling a wilderness of water,
water disguised, gone under,
hiding beneath the levels.
Peat-cloaked, this water's
palomino, pewter, potent.

Fifteen miles of road, a tarmac torc.
Buildings are few, crouch at the fringe
with the air of trespassers –
self-conscious, sagging shacks,
red-brick rows of peat-workers,
untidy farms encroaching
like lice on the shaggy coat
of a great beast. The bog
breathes, renews, moves,
is their warden, their time-keeper
impressing upon them their impermanence.

Snowdrops. A house was here,
half-way habitat at the wood's edge
poised between wilderness and wild.
The white surprise among dereliction –
uncountable clusters, minute nuns
praying in a weed garden. Witnesses
to births and deaths, the rise and fall
of structures. Moss has crept
where quoins once were; lichen claims
a crumbling fence; hart's tongue fern
flames in the hearth-place.

Another house gone blind, abandoned.
One Sixties car and a lorry left,
rusty as red sphagnum. Their grills grin,
deathmasks of chrome. Dormice-dens,
gorse gains ground under their chassis,
moss embeds their wheels. Rooted,
these vehicles warn the Star-Trek people
(sad fairground wintering here)
*travel on, gather no moss.*

I come alone, savouring solitude,
seeking to slice through time,
feel inner frost melt,
reinhabit my own space.
The past is an eye-blink away –
the peat an archive, ages packed
underground; a tangible reservoir.

*Give Way!* The notice blares at a crossroads.
*Go back!* The caution ricochets through dead heather.
*No further, no further! This is not your place!*

## The Interior

Beyond the last holding, outbuildings,
the nested Range Rover, wire fencing,
a paddock where Jacob sheep graze,
this black track leads to the cuttings.

I am stepping ahead of myself
over the mantle of mosses,
passing a sprawl of bramble
where beetles seethe,
passing ivory stumps of pines,
their roots pre-Roman.
The bog, with its inner sea,
has memory. I touch the peat,
the past pulsing under my palm.

Now I'm stumbling after my shadow,
see the sparrowhawk see the shrew –
their union a matter of moments.

I leap tussocks, avoid brilliant green –
mossy invitation to drown –
recalling nineteenth-century turfmen's finds:

the skeleton of a woman, her skull a blown egg;
the man, face-down, partly covered
in flesh, brought up from the Bronze Age;
the lad, his wooden stool and leather apron,
in sitting position, surprised by death.
Three bodies, pickled like plants,
buried again in consecrated ground.
I stare at black earth, robbed of its secrets,
almost hear spades slucking, slapping.
Time makes us losers in our turn.

Across the bog, mist seeks a resting place
like windblown thistledown. Behind the gauze
recruits for the Great War line up
at rifle ranges, fire at target butts
of peat, march past cuts like trenches
in No Man's Land. Behind the smoke
a crashed Wellington burns, nose diving
on bombing practice, killing five.
Behind the veil pale flutterings, the Shoot
of waders, pheasants, a licensed kill.

I think of Nietzsche –
*if you gaze for long into an abyss,*
*the abyss gazes also into you...*

beneath the black glaze
might be chasm or catacomb.

This imperceptible merging – earth
with water, present with past,
season into season.

## The Peat-Cutters

They know the calendar by the mosses' hues:
in winter, the slow erasure of colour
frost-blanched to tones of ash and oat
where the kestrel keeps faith with the field-mouse,
the sedge shivers in a raking wind,
low moan of advancing snow.
White-out. The hummocks of the bog
are a sea of frozen breakers.

At melt-time the peat-cutters return:
their sabots squelch, their spades slit,
slick through. They lift embedded stones
where water seeps, the level rising,
reversing desiccation. New cuttings rough-hewn –
each one at night a trough of stars.

*

Some evenings, stumbling home in mist
their shapes emerge; others blow whistles
when dark falls on fog, the bog sucks.
Say bog, think of bodies – soil's store
in an acid hold preserving –
perhaps, too, the bones of mammoths.
Peat-cutters fear they'll slice through flesh.

One's convinced he's seen Judge Jeffreys,
heard his haunting horn, horses' hammer,
shriek of fox, like mandrakes torn.
Baron of Wem, his estate 'The Law',
'Bloodfingers' Jeffreys dealt in death,
gibbets gorged with Sedgemoor rebels
trapped like flies in the sundew.

*

Below zero: the earth again ice-locked –
cuttings grow new skin; twigs balance upright.
Peat-workers stare at sculpted ground, white roots
tapping down ten thousand years. These black zones
could be an entrance to the Underworld
where Charon waits on the bog-bordered Styx.

They stack their turves, feed some to the shredder,
mindful of fingers, arms, how old Joe died.
Yet Spring's sneaking in like a svelte grass-snake,
the sphagnum's now greening, birds linking song.
Soon, orchid, rosemary, bog asphodel
will follow emerald, their colour of hope.

# The Women of Whixall

*Margaret Platt, Wife of Jim*

My washing line's slung from the pollarded poplar –
Jim isn't really a practical man –
good with the spade, he digs for our future,
at home he's makeshift, his fittings fall down.
I bring in iced washing, sharp as Jim's blade,
crucified shirts, briefs in bright blocks,
baby clothes cut out of white card,
and all those assorted stalactite socks.

*

*Barbara Harrison's Dream of Water-Snakes*

I saw their golden bodies water-weaving
slim, sinuous beside my sliding ship.
I felt their fire-flash, flaring
as they slipped into my blood
swimming through my roots to tips of hair.

They coiled behind my eyes,
came curling through my thoughts,
circled my soul as if a tourniquet –

they flowed out through my flesh,
I see them now, in their own element,
black water-worms in slimy knots.
Their golden skins became my albatross.

*

16

## Agnes Morris – Making Whixall Wreaths

*Custom dating back to 1915*

'The holly and the ivy
When they are both full grown…'
Clipped from the bough each year
from the same trees in Shropshire's russet crown,
the prickly harvest falls reluctantly
into our hands. Dark green shine
for Christmas wreaths, softened by sphagnum,
top moss dried, arranged on frames.
With fingers increasingly tender
we weave in kitchens in December.

*

## Judith Price, by Anne, her Niece

This horizontal line –
feet to head, ward, corridor,
long tarmac to flat fields,
a motorway, the inevitable horizon.

This person, part of a bed –
she tells me her feet are cold,
asks where is the furniture,
why does the room have no walls?

This space disorientates, grows,
an ever-expanding bubble
bisected by a horizontal line –
feet to head, part of a bed.
She is a thin river dividing fens
she is a baby held out in a bath
she is the child in a cradle
this is her cot, with bars down.

Once she had trespassed, laughing
to bring me bluebells – her god-daughter-niece,
the child she never had. Once she caught buses
alone, adventuring to town cafés.

Snowlight:
she wants to cup it in her hands,
asks for snowsongs, canticles of praise –
still a celebrant of life
she jokes with the priest
*And give those plants some Holy Water too!*
I hear with surprise of her love of yachts,
unspoken, except for birthday-card pictures.

On her burial morning, I see in the clouds
a single yacht, white sail winging:
there she goes, waving to me
as she crosses her horizon.

## Survivor

Shuffling to his shed, Tommy Pitt
sifts the ragged peat-loaves, slots
each one in the shredder, sorts out
knotty roots, some bone-white,
while the rich grain shoots down
to a rising mound, tawny tobacco-heap.
Memories, impossible to shred, are knitted
into his mind's tissue, the grown-over scars
of World War Two. Today his shattered leg
aches like a limb in chill armour.

*Move on. Move over. Move him here…*
*Taken from the tank, lowered to the stretcher.*
*Steady now… the swaying and jerking*
*across ruts to a copse. The waiting in darkness*
*and then a deeper dark.*

His shed is isled in mist
slow to dissolve into the morning,
slipping him back to Normandy fields,
fog and foe, brambles booby-trapped.
*Two haystacks move. He opens fire –*
*shedding straw they fire back.*
*His tank rips open in a metal-burst…*

The rat-tat-tat of the shredder –
but his ears are deadened to the sound,
his deafness doesn't matter on the Moss.
Another cart arrives, the peat stacked high…
outside he leans against a tree,
fingers the bark like a scab.

## Beginner

Taking my tranny –
no-one will see –
must have company,
the BBC!
Diggin' on the Moss
no-one will hear –
there might be the Beatles,
they're the gear!
Or the Rollin' Stones maybe –
my group therapy.
Don't wanna end up
like Uncle Tommy.

Gonna leave here
perhaps to Abergavenny
with my pal Kevin.
Kev's got ideas.

Been at the peat a year
a year too many.
Dad wants me to work
Mum wants me near.
No jobs around here –
I'll get away, get clear
perhaps try the Army
but
I don't wanna end up
like Uncle Tommy.

## Dragonfly Weather

Return. I rejoice in dragonfly weather
tracking paths towards the centre
to oblongs of fallen sky
clouds floating in cuttings,
my quest the white-faced dragonfly.

Peace here is
     plop of vole, head-first, from the side
     an adder sunning near heather
     brown hare nibbling moorgrass
     thin songs of curlew and lapwing
     large heath butterflies sipping nectar
the silent skating of the great raft spider –
he mounts his reflection, waits
still as a twig, for surface vibrations,
catches the unwary waterboatman.

I wait, still as a heron, anticipate.
And out from sheltering sphagnum, lured by light
they come on the glass of their wings,
white-faced dragonflies whose faces shine
resembling us at dusk. Domino darts
drawn to the honey traps.

The sundew opens red lips
succulent entrapment in its bed
of moss. Upward long leaves curl
offering sweetness, stickum
enticing dragonflies, any flies.
Sprawled in a boggy boudoir
the sundew's a passive killer
like this peatland, swallowing.

In such horizontals, desire for verticals.
I see a stack of peat blocks drying out
piled high, like forgotten books,
old Bibles bound in black leather,
reminding me of sixteenth-century texts
Bishop Morgan's translation into Welsh
a Bible for the people in their language.
Yet some words escape their renderings
flow as the tongues of waterfalls
never the same twice.

Comes the shadow of a kestrel crossways
over the hummocks, breaking and renewing.

I have drawn back the dark coverlet,
gazed for long into the underside of water,
studied my own shadow.

Time now to retreat, leaving the twilight
to twilight's creatures, leaving
the bog wrapped in itself.

# Histories

# TERRA INCOGNITA

Across the high moors to Pentrefoelas,
sunset already claiming western hills,
the road ahead razoring through heather –

his red scarf flared in my driving mirror,
I saw his beetle head, dull black leather:
the distance closed, he seemed part of my car.

Accelerating, I pulled ahead, clear
of his front wheel. Again he drew too near,
daring the switchback of the coming miles

unwinding in front of us, like film spools.
Towards a ruined building on a rise
we raced as one in a dual slipstream

startling a flight of swallows in a cwm,
dipping down to a marshpool near the rim
of the narrow road, rounding two tight bends.

Where the curve straightened he swerved – in seconds
at my side, riding parallel for yards.
In tandem we approached the next hairpin.

I braked for him to overtake (or win)
and caught the heady fumes from his engine.
He revved, roared off, leaning into the twist.

Next I saw him hurtling up the hillcrest
dwindling into a dot, a spume of dust.
Five miles of moor and marsh, no other cars

to where fieldslopes begin, the fringe of farms;
and on the skyline, beneath early stars,
the signature of Snowdon, indigo.

Reaching a tilting lane, banked with willow
I saw a signpost, and his bike below –
seeming at rest, it nestled in the hedge;

further on, a river disguised as ditch –
and there a car embedded in the bridge,
unnatural outcrop of the slate and stone.

Nowhere the rider, driver, anyone;
no time for an ambulance to have come.
I searched, found only splintered metal, glass

the bike's red paint in flakes upon the grass,
a raven's feather fallen as it passed,
the sunset now a gash between night cloud.

# CONVOLVULUS

Mid-July, the bindweed high in the hedge –
a 'tatty' hedge Nain calls it, sitting in the yard,
tilting her kitchen chair, as sunlight pinks the sandstone
of soot-crusted walls. The tall house casts its shadow
over the dusty privet, shades Nain's face.

She tells me of the day before –
the large white coach packed with mothers
winding through Flintshire lanes, higher into hills
by Halkyn mountain, to the sheltering greystone Friary –
and how, uncrumpling themselves, the mothers stood
in the peace of Pantasaph, a peace so palpable
they felt they could touch, hold it in their hands,
bring some home with the Holy Pictures.

Each one chingled a rosary, processing uphill,
kneeling on the bare ground of the path
at every Station of the Cross, until at last
they formed a circle around the crucifix,
huge, tethered to the hill-top like a mast.
Here they prayed, made secret requests.
Nain wouldn't tell me hers, but smiled
whispering as if the wind would hear –
'A poet, Francis Thompson, once stayed there.
We were shown the window of his room.'

Afterwards, downhill to Holywell,
a blessing at St Winefride's ceaseless spring.
Some mothers wept in the candle-lit shrine,
clear waters calling, reflecting inner wounds;
and constantly rising from the source
its bubbles seemed, Nain thought,
a waterchain of souls, renewing forever.

I wanted to bring her flowers, plucked convolvulus
but the white chalices folded in my hand.


*Nain: grandmother (North Wales)*

26

# TRAPEZE

Drawn by the pulse of music
in a sunlit Zurich square
we see child acrobats in air –
bright blossoms tossed
from their parents' arms.
High on the swinging trapeze
they perform their part, babes
with an assured yet tremulous art.

We are a crowd transformed
to audience, welded as we watch
the patterned movements, bonded
by the children's dangerous ease
daring to dive into space –
their bodies schooled, yet
not quite submissive.

Dissecting the air with arcs
this geometry of children
transcends language
imprints the sky,
their last uncoiling curve
a question mark
on the implacable blue.

## COUCHETTE – ZURICH TO BRUXELLES

Pulling out on time, to the half-second,
leaving Zurich, its frieze of interior Alps,
the night train curves north to Basel.
I watch from the corridor slits of last light
diminishing in August midnight.
Into the gloom of the four-slot cabin
I find my couchette on the bottom level,
crouch like a chinchilla on a ledge.
Trying to write by torchlight I'm aware
of other travellers on shelves above
wrapped in thin sheets of Belgian cotton.

The train rushes on in deepening night
its left-right rhythm a lullaby
until near Basel the screaming of brakes
then utter stillness in a desert of rails.
I hear murmuring from the upper couchette,
see a bronzed hand reach out, carve a kiss
in air; while opposite a smaller hand extends
connects with his in a lovers' clasp,
their arms and hands a loop across the cabin
like those low chains in stately homes
keeping viewers out of special rooms.

I flashback to Zurich and two lovers
lying side by side in a long embrace
inside their makeshift house of plastic sheets
on the perfect lawn of the Landesmuseum.
His bandaged arm reached out, enfolding her,
they'd clung together in a final ecstasy
drug-doomed and dying as the sunlight struck,
gilding for a moment their see-through roof.
Later, their separate journeys – on stretchers
in an ambulance flashing them away.

The train streaks on, magnetised to Bruxelles,
and I watch dawn's levelling grey
over miles of mixed suburbs.
Steel lines cross, re-cross, criss-cross
like lives that for a brief while intersect
then veer away on different tracks.
We slide into the waiting mouth of the Gare
walk away towards the rest of our lives.

# LINDOW MAN

*A late Iron Age Celt found in the Cheshire peat-bog,*
*Lindow Moss, near Wilmslow, August 1984.*
*Now on display in the British Museum.*

Young man, we know your features
recreated from the bogland skull.
Your unblemished body was well-fed,
not scarred either by work or harp-strings.
Celtic sacrifice, brought by barbarous rites
to this final nurture, your last meal
the burnt bannock. Barley grains inside you
and mistletoe pollen, surviving centuries,
now witness to your druidic death.
Was it ordained for Beltain, this offering
of your perfect body to the Gods –
propitiation, in hope of a rich harvest?

Prince or priest, reared for this moment
your life a preparation for this death,
an honour to appease the thirsty Gods –
for Tarainis, the shattering head-blows,
for Esus, the garrotte and slit throat,
for Teuttades, the face-down drowning.

You bring the harvest of yourself
to our fact-hungry times, yield
a cerebral feast from your stored existence,
salt sanctuary violated.
Today we file by your glass coffin,
stare at an historical artefact –
your contorted, leathery body.
Yes, you have taken us forward
to the past, our god Knowledge
is well satisfied. But I wish for you
the privacy of your peat-bog grave.

# CAPTAIN FITZROY'S GAMBLE

*(for Malcolm Bradley)*

Something about Darwin's nose and brow
alarmed me. Even so, I selected him –
a natural choice – considering his ability,
his unbounded vigour at twenty-two,
what I needed for *The Beagle*, a voyage,
among other things, to prove the Bible right.

All went well until Rio. Our first quarrel.
His first journey into the tropical forest,
returning foolishly fired up, having witnessed
the condition of the native Indian.
I warned him to calm down – after all,
slavery's part of the natural order,
a fact he certainly should understand.

I ordered him off my ship –
indeed, he was already packed to go.
Then, providentially, my temper cooled.
I called him back, and he came.

Divine intervention perhaps. At Tierra del Fuego
we were inland, a hundred miles from *The Beagle*,
our boat tethered offshore. We were camped
high in the forest, among the Fuegians –
people more like animals than men.
When the glacier cracked, hurtling into the sea,
Darwin saved us, securing our boat, our escape.
In gratitude I named this peak
'Mount Darwin'.

# THE FIRST PRIVATE CALL

*14th January 1878*

What will they ask me to open next, I wonder?
Last month a new dock, before that a Town Hall.
Now this contraption. Not open it exactly.
Try it out. Of course they know what they're doing –
experiments elsewhere – America, no doubt.
But I'm to make this first private call. Connected
to Osborne Cottage for a trial communication.

*Leave it there*, I ordered. *All go out.*
*Let me get used to it. It won't explode.*
They backed out, giving me these moments
to think out what I'm going to say.

How far can words travel? Travelling words.
Voices whirling down wires, across space.
And life already sufficiently complicated!
This is where one speaks. Hold the tube close
to the ear, as the Professor instructed.
Most extraordinary. A mystery.
What would my beloved have thought of it, I wonder?
Inventions his field, dear heart.

To send out words, hear voices from afar,
converse perhaps with spirits waiting there
(not all go on to some distant heaven) –
I've heard of lingering souls, those cruelly cut off
like dearest Albert. Often I've felt his presence
especially at Windsor, just outside his room.
I sense he's somewhere close. Could I call him?
Would he answer along the wire?
They'll think I'm crazed – my great sadness
always worse at Christmas and New Year.

Better here – Osborne soothes me. The sea air.
And this instrument, brought for a demonstration
intended to amuse me, I understand.
The Professor predicts a network of installations.
How useful this could be at the Palace –
summoning carriages for tedious guests,
terminating those endless conversations.

But only at the Palace. Never here. One must be private.
Now they're coming back into the Council Room.
What am I to say? How will I begin? Good evening?
Sir Thomas and Mary Biddulph are you there?

## TO D.H. LAWRENCE

You, who all your life
were crossing borders,
whose 'come-from' included
a grandfather's Derbyshire roots,
freewheeled in youth, cycling
from Eastwood down to the Erewash,
climbed the darker-than-limestone tors
of Matlock, marvelling at crinoids, finding
fresh perspectives in space and time.
You walked in woodland of sessile oak,
one with the life of its creatures, yet
aware of black cloisters nearby, smelling
the coaldust which choked your father.

Sure of a new world within, travelling
beyond the country of your heart,
you could not have foreseen
your permanent arrival in the sun –
bright mountains above Taos,
heights over the Rio Grande,
among hibiscus flowers, blue balsam pines –
Kiowa Ranch where Frieda settled
your ashes, carried across continents
(deathmask made at Vence), to be
forever part of England in a foreign pasture.
Mexico, a long way from Matlock.

# THE BLACK CHAIR OF BIRKENHEAD

*An Ode to Hedd Wyn (1887–1917)*

Not in green Wales this Eisteddfod,
the National 1917 in soot-dark Birkenhead.
Far from your mountain moors, Trawsfynydd,
the clear streams, sweet river Prysor,
flock, farm and family –
yet not so far as Passchendaele.

That September the trees in the Park
were already leafed in red
when from the stage your name was called,
the heraldic call across the massive tent,
a ritual summons to claim the bardic prize.
Archdruid Dyfed, Lloyd George, Leverhulme, knew
from that audience you would not rise.

The empty Chair enveloped in black,
your absence filling the auditorium
told of Armageddon
as you lay in Flanders, six weeks dead.

Given into your family's keeping
the dark-draped throne on a cart
was processed the long lane to Yr Ysgwrn.
Crested with flaring dragons
its fine oak craftsman-carved
by a Belgian refugee of Borough Road.

*Hedd Wyn* was the Bardic name of Ellis Humphrey Evans of Trawsfynydd,
Merionethshire, killed in France, 31 July 1917 in the Third Battle of Ypres
(Passchendaele).
The Royal National Eisteddfod, 2–9 September 1917, was held in Birken-
head Park. Hedd Wyn won the Chair with his *awdl* (ode) on the set theme
'The Hero'.
The Chair was carved by Mr Van Fletereran of Malines, Belgium, a refugee
then living in Borough Road, Birkenhead.

# FOR THE CENTENARY OF WILFRED OWEN
(1893–1918)

## 1.

*'The sea is rising... and the world is sand.'*
                Wilfred Owen, 1916

In Milton Road tonight, a boy playing in the summer light
wears a crash helmet, manoeuvres his bike.
Down the slope he rides, shoots a frown at me,
aware that I'm staring at Fifty-One –
Victorian villa, the Birkonian home
of the Owens (Tom, Susan, four children).
From here Wilfred, proud of his uniform,
smartly set off to Whetstone Lane and school.
A time that was nurturing, unriven:
Sunday School at Claughton, walks to Bidston –
woods and windmill he knew well; also Meols
(his cousins' house 'Dorfold'). For young Harold
brotherly protection, inventions, games.
And boyhood joys – swimming at local baths,
riding a horse beside wild Mersey waves;
his pleasure in learning, crafting first poems.

Ten years from here, a lifetime further on,
nerves shattered by shell-fire near St Quentin,
did he, perhaps, think back to Birkenhead,
recall the mothering hours at Milton Road
where a boy, tonight, is riding his bike in the summer light.


## 2. War Exhibition
(Williamson Art Gallery, Birkenhead)

*75th anniversary of the Armistice, 1918*

In this calm gallery, built between two wars,
each viewer embarks on a journey
to the Western Front.

Here in a dug-out, the chalky mud dried out,
sits Lieutenant Owen. Sandbag-shielded
wearing full battledress, he tightly grips
his pen. At the Front Line, in a lull,
he's writing letters home or drafting
verbal photographs of battle –
truths of suffering he's seen,
truths war artists were forbidden to convey.
> *They are dying again at Beaumont Hamel*
> *which already, in 1916, was cobbled with skulls.*

Paintings show British soldiers at bayonet practice,
trying gas masks, filling water bottles,
bringing in prisoners like winter cattle.
They go over the top, remain intact.
One smokes a pipe, another plays an accordion,
some are eating, a few have bandaged wounds.
> *Of whose blood lies yet crimson on my shoulder*
> *where his head was... I must not now write.*

Commissioned art promotes *the old Lie*
(depicting the British dead prohibited)
the corpses and mutilated are all German.
A crump shell explodes, stretcher-bearers –
ants across earth's carcass – advance
> *the ground all crawling and wormy*
> *with wounded bodies.*

And here comes reveller Death, in a cloak,
striding over duckboards, yet halting awed
before a blown-off boot.

*The quotations are from the 'Collected Letters of Wilfred Owen' (1967),*
*by kind permission of Oxford University Press. The visual art referred to*
*includes a mixed media Trench Scene by Jim Whelan (commissioned for*
*the Exhibition); prints by Eric Kennington, Frank Brangwyn, Paul Nash,*
*John Nash, Harold Sandys Williamson and Percy Smith.*

# MALCOLM LOWRY IN PARADISE STREET

*(Lowry: a red fox, in North Country dialect)*

All his life he fled from sadistic nannies –
fearing flagellation, rain-tub torture –
initiated early into fleshly fantasy,
at five, with big brother to Paradise Street,
the small anatomical museum. Turnstile click –
V.D. to be the tick in his mind –
seeing the syphilitic sick, models a raree show,
physical parables of punishment – the sins
of the fathers on the children… the children's children.
Grotesques in glass bottles, like the deformed puppies
he'd seen that week, curled into each other
concealed in a corner at Caldy Farm.

All his life he assumed disguises,
fleeing from twin tyrannies – the pen, the bottle –
sailing out early in ultramarine waters,
composing jazz, curled in the womb of his ukulele;
even at Cambridge fearing the spirochaete
he'd corkscrew yet another bottle,
unable to heal the lesions in his mind.

From Mexico to Vancouver, exiled from alcohol,
secure in a beach shanty, talking only to fishermen,
netted by draft after draft of his novel,
he was flayed by his own words, creating
a drunken protagonist, watching
the way light slatted and dissolved
on the walls of his shack. His brilliance flared,
his shack flamed. Vulpine, always moving on,
feted, then forgotten, he was haunted
by coastal light across a Wirral golf course,
crowds applauding a schoolboy champion,
a split tanker's black seepage in the Mersey,
the pickled spectres of Paradise Street.

Under the volcano of his own pysche
he erupted, ran to earth,
making his final escape –
the tray of tablets, the broken gin bottle,
'Death by Misadventure'.

## ONCE A MONTH

Beneath the suburban hill, near Wembley's domes
the city line sneaks, slither-speeding through.
Her cries obliterate its midday rhythms,
rise to the rafters, bisect the air –
*They're writhing round my feet! Please come!*
I cross the hall to her bed-sit door,
she's standing rigidly, hands to her ears –
*They're tangling in my hair, around my throat!*
I hold her – Lona Truding – as she shakes,
smooth her cropped head, its gloss of raven dye,
wrap her close in a dressing gown.
*There's nothing there,* I reassure.
*Look down. You're free to move.*
She follows me, sob-shuffling to my room.

Next week she's playing Beethoven's Fifth,
complains again about the dusty staircase,
asks why the bin-men haven't come,
curses as she trudges up the path –
and I know she's recovered from the visitation,
her once-monthly reunion with her past,
the lost relatives, her fiancé taken to Treblinka.

## FESTIVE INITIATION

Behind glass, in the corner cupboard,
circles of gold, rose-rimmed,
large and small moons.
Unlocking her wedding-ware
for the once-yearly ceremony of use,
she carried each one like a fragile child
to its ritual place on the elongated table.
This bone-thin reverence, part of Christmas –
chill plates I feared to touch, or taste
their pale offering of poultry flakes
or fork the stubborn marble-pickles.

Within the parlour's gloom, a coffin-shape –
the rosewood pianola,
his paid-for pride's possession.
He took me in to listen, opened the long lid,
laid in Rachmaninov in a perforated roll.
Adjusting coat and sleeves he pumped the pedals,
mock finger-movements making music.
At last my turn. He let me try with Liszt –
I barely reached the pedals, stretching, pushing
to release Beethoven, press on through Bach.
In imaginary concert halls I triumphed
with Mozart, Schumann, Chopin – until,
legs locked, I was half-carried home.

Sometimes now, when cycling up steep gradients,
I pedal to Ravel, the relentless *Bolero*,
and think of Grandad, his rosewood coffin-music-box;
or glimpsing wild roses in the hedges,
I remember Grandma, her cold cabinet of gold.

## THE BORROWED ROOM

Accustomed year after year to her presence,
slow movements, suppressed moans,
this room wants to eject me.

The walls seem to wince when I rush about.
Her blue armchair smothers my muse,
breathes enormously *rest-sleep, rest-sleep.*

Tall windows form a bay of light
but also a barrier impossible to breach,
keeping the gleaming day outside.

Pale as ash this ceiling, covered with her sighs.
The final loss her cat, twin at eighty-nine,
white fur and bones thinning, eye-sight failing.

Her bed retains me, marooned in her shape.
The mirror gives me back her face. I look
for myself, lost beneath her filigree of wrinkles.

Lulled into lethargy, I wait for departure.
My clothes are sagging on the wooden hangers
in a wardrobe smelling of 1923.

On the last morning I slowly pack my cases,
pick up the fallen pen, the blank paper,
my unplayed radio near her cold china clock.

Leaving, I notice white hairs on my jacket,
the cat basket empty in a corner,
her dust merged with mine on the mirror.

# BEES

A summer of signs after spring's disasters –
March snows and the house in flames,
relationships cracking in the gutted rooms.

Pilot bees found the yielding hole,
pierced the apex to the space beneath,
discovered a cavity wall fit for a queen.

June's sudden warmth brought restoration,
new plaster, floorboards, ceilings, doors.
We reclaimed the bedroom, the King-size bed.

Above the new ceiling a chain-saw sound
cohorts hovering through the lofty dark;
preparation of nurseries and the Queen installed.

Like newly-weds, we were adjusting,
plastering old wounds, honeying what was scorched.
But invasively each day, a disturbance,

bees colonising, busy with brood-combs
in the roof now theirs and ours. We heard
the dark swirl of their comings and goings,

found their dead on the drive, black eyes like beads,
wings a white shroud. Of our own lives we knew
that which was burnt was not purified.

The house cries out, night floorboards vocal;
each year the bees blaze, our hidden blisters itch,
we share the honey, accept the sting.

# AUGURY

*Blodeuwedd, The Mabinogion*

Tall bedraggled pines, the day's incessant rain,
early nightfall and a river-road. You plunged
swift whiteness into the stream of light
intent on some small creature spotlit
on the camber, caught in my car's beams.
I felt your winged death impacting,
kept steady as you were woven in
becoming one with metal, rubber.
Not an everyday extinction. Born
of need, and one I saw as portent.
Next morning, cautious, tense,
I looked at last around the rim
of tyre, wheel-arch, finding you
translated
from feathers into fur into flowers.

And death followed three-fold.

Last night, one year later, your return
waiting on the wires, intent
close to the cottage eaves.
Your ululation as I arrived,
how you opened your wings like a cloak
to enfold me; how you became
one with the moon's translucency
your call dwindling into the blackness of Bryn Alyn.
Today, on the slate path to our door, I find
three gifts – your feather, white-tipped,
a dead but perfect fieldmouse,
a sprig of broom.

44

# POEMS FOR PAINTINGS

*David Garrick as Richard III, by William Hogarth (1743)*

## Garrick's Richard

*'For Dickon, thy master, is bought and sold.'*
Shakespeare, *Richard III*

This actor's eloquent eyes, gentle features
are closer to the real Richard Neville
than Shakespeare's depiction of a villain.

No crouchback either, but straight and soldierly
(as witnessed by many). Political caricature,
Tudor concoction, perpetuated in poetry
in a play to please a Queen. Those deaths –
assassinations? The young princes, his nephews
sickening in the Tower. The blame on his shoulders.

No snake in the grass, but serpentine,
stretched out by Hogarth in a sinuous line,
the artist seeing beauty in this shape
and in his friend, the convincing actor
who here is surely pleading Richard's innocence?

*Isabella, by John Everett Millais (1848–49)*

## Dining with the Enemy

How will we do it, topple this schemer?
He's having his *last* meal at our table.
Our young sister's caught by this sly charmer –
courting her will bring him more than trouble,
Lorenzo, mere apprentice to our trade;
fool Isabella, so beguiled, in love.
Their love? see my falcon tearing a dove –
with my brother I'll rip him from her side.

She knows her family needs her to wed high –
a noble of Siena, bringing wealth,
securing our future, should trade run dry.
Oh, Isabella, loyalty's not felt.
You've forced us to devise a deadly plan –
Emilio broods on it as he sips wine.

Each in the other is so closely bound
(she hangs upon his wily whisperings)
neither notices that I kick her hound.
Lorenzo gives her sliced blood oranges –
emblem of his fate. None can halt its course.
Near the Arno's bank, north of Firenze,
in thick forest we'll chop him from his horse.
This will please our uncle Corleone.

*Faithful unto Death, by Edward J. Poynter (1865)*

## One Summer Day

I remember the time exactly.
We were just finishing a meal,
nectarines and grapes in our hands,
white wine in sparkling goblets.
We were sitting in the garden of Julia Felix
under the shade of her new verandah –
she, with pride, showing us her gold snake ring,
the presents brought back by her husband
from Greece. Another ring, a cameo of her profile,
her tresses exquisite in sardonyx. As she held it up,
the filigreed gold and creamy stone against a sky
as blue as lapis lazuli, we stared
fixed by her white hand, the gleaming ring
and a dark fungus of cloud behind,
growing rapidly, its core of flame spurting.

The ground shook, our goblets scattered –
we were running in panic, rocks raining down.
Constantly the cloud threw out its destruction
like a God vengeful against our summer world,
the sumptuous sinning. Choking, we escaped,
taking boats south to Amalfi, where we heard
today of the ash burying Pompeii.

Our cousin Marcello was on sentry duty – we saw him
as we fled, called to him, but he didn't hear us,
standing against the orange glare. At his post.
What a privilege to die that way!
But, sad to say, we lost our faithful Paurus
chained, guarding the door of our villa.
We will come to Roma, dear Father,
be assured. We send our love to Nerina.
Your son, Petronius, at Positano.

*The Scapegoat by W. Holman Hunt (1854)*

## The Scapegoat

*(for Frank Milner)*

*'And the Goat shall bear upon him all the iniquities*
*unto a land not inhabited.'*
                    Leviticus XVI 22

**1.**

This goat's a ragged beast
his harmless horns bound with scarlet –
they wreathed him in red on Atonement Day
to carry away their sins, bear the stain.
Now, goaded into this wilderness, he stands
desolate on the Dead Sea shore.
Almost sinking in the sand, as if weighed down
by a cross, he stumbles, thirst-racked
near the salt water, tideless sea of Sodom.

Will his scarlet turn to white
signifying sins forgiven? Not until
his bones whiten the white sand
and his bleached garland is time's token.


**2.**

*'a scene of beautifully arranged horrible wilderness.'*
                    Holman Hunt, *Diary, 1854*

In Jerusalem, Hunt bought a white goat
packed onto a cart, with trestles, tents
for his camp at Osdoom on the sea of sinners.
There, measuring distances, proportions
he tethered his model on the saline shore.

Precision in his laying on of paint:
foreground details the appropriate skulls,
animal skeletons strewn along the marsh;
middle distance the fishless sea, water without rhythm;
background a barrier of hills, stained purple.

All was accurate around the white space,
blank shape of the scapegoat, outlined
but not yet depicted, though day after day
the beast stood, fixed in position.

Did the artist feel a weight of guilt
when, in merciless heat, salt air
this goat, red ribbons in his horns, sank dying
to the sand, like a slaughtered bull
under the torero's exact point?

*Ville d'Avray, White Houses,*
*by Georges Pierre Seurat (1882)*

## White Houses

*(for Gill Curry)*

Someone else's secrets shuttered here
behind pale walls, the screen of trees.
Security in squares, oblongs –
no hint in this grouping
of nuances of lives, relationships.
Not his concern, otherness
not what he's after, this artist
himself a man of secrets; his stance
from across a cornfield, distance
yielding a safer perspective.

Do these leafy suburbs remind him
how his father withdrew, solitary,
to the fringes of Paris, an allotment?
His seeing brush avoids
engagement with eyes, mouths.
His quest is to dissect the heart
of colour, break open its secret,
dissolve into vibrant seeds, exact
in close coupling.

Of Madeleine Knobloch, his model,
mistress, wife, he gave no hint,
nor of their son Pierre-Georges –
undisclosed to family, friends.
Divisionist technique,
his people part of his pattern, static
as these white houses of Ville d'Avray.

# The Land Within

A Sequence of Poems
to
MARY WEBB

# THE LAND WITHIN

## 1. Child of Spring

### Leighton Lodge, 25th March 1881

First day of Spring,
gleam of Ladyday
on the Severn, coiling
beneath greenfleeced Wrekin.

At Leighton hedgebanks
freshly set with primrose clusters,
sharp spears of leaves
tightly furled, piercing
into the light, into clarity
of rain-rinsed air. Here burgeons
the song of returning migrants

ringing from tall trees
reaching every recess
greeting the child on the threshold.

Born into her heritage –
nature's green-gold gates
flung wide.

## 2. Her Shropshire Eden

### The Grange, Much Wenlock, 1882–96

The tutor father, his elfin daughter
delicate, on tip-toe to see nestlings,
to see foxcubs cuffing, dormouse
on a corn-stalk, damselflies on the rushes
of her own round pond. On tip-toe

asking questions, endless questions,
*why* and *how* and *when* –
his *precious bane*,
his *dear little girlie*.

She is nurtured on Milton, Wordsworth,
Shakespeare, Virgil, the Bible.
Her father, of Prince Llywelyn's line,
face of a Welsh shepherd,
eyes far-seeing, grey-blue as cwm-water,
his mind stored with riches.
He initiates her in *nature's occult script*
the secrets of seeds
      the lore of the honey bee
the meaning of the cross
      in the heart of flowers.
And she is the wild rose
        hanging on the thorn.


**'Nature's Mystick Book'**
      Andrew Marvell

Dawn-walking to see the shadows
of sunrise, giant silhouettes
cast across meadows,
trees bowing down to the sun.

She is one with the clover
unfolding at morning,
one with the bee
visiting the clover,

she is there at twilight
watching white clover close
almost imperceptibly
its praying petal hands

she perceives each
*pale shadow of a gesture*
knows *the hidden scent of every tree*
untangles *the ravelled sweetness*
in the summer air, discerns
*emanations of moss*
the redolence of rock, learns
*the perfume thrushes smell,*
*which makes their song as keen as pain.*

Building for frogs a cool little house
of stones at the rim of the pond,
making a sanctuary for anything wounded,
a hospital in the house
for the rabbit with the ripped ear
for the dying fledglings torn by a cat
for the cat savaged by a dog
for the dog shot by mistake
in the rookery of the Grange
shot by a family guest,
filled with lead meant for the rooks,
the gentle dog sketched by her father
in the stable yard, near the fig tree,
where she danced and twirled.
The rifle shots that rended the air
ended her peace

and later, after the hunt swept by
under Wenlock Edge
she would grieve for the fox
finding one that escaped
the jaws of the hounds
but not before their wild tearing
of fine nerve, soft tissue –
not before the kill that would come
slowly in agony. And so
*the death-pack roamed*
let loose in her life.

Bonfire night. Turnip lanterns.
Baked potatoes and chestnuts.
Cook's best for the guests –
          all her little guests from the cottages
from the damp dwellings of consumptives
she visited and sorrowed over –
          all the children on her list
brought up to the Grange in the carriage.
Always this yearning to assuage.

Gifts around the Christmas spruce
for every poor child of Wenlock,
spiced cake, sweets, fruit –
and the magic of 'little Miss Meredith's play'
acted by her father and servants.

Late Spring, snow lingering on Shropshire's hills,
Mr Meredith and his eldest, off to Church Stretton.
Riding in the pony-trap along the wooded Edge
he names for her the distant heights, relates
their legends, folklore. Heroic Caractacus
of Caer Caradoc, Wild Edric of the Stiperstones,
satanic occupant of the Devil's Chair,
unresting ghosts of coppies and pools –
          *voices calling a long way off.*
And on the Edge, the sheer cliff
where a Cavalier evaded Roundheads
leaping his horse into air – a man hunted down
like a fox, his horse killed by the fall...
          *claimed by the death-pack.*

Enthralled, in the charmed circle,
she begins her patternings
ideas, words into stories, sonnets.

## 3. The Bible of Pain

*The Woodlands, Stanton-on-Hine Heath, 1896–1902*

Here, in the walled garden
here, beneath the bent-with-age mulberry,
surrounded by pale pastures
she listens to the first lambs,
their calls wavering like falling blossom,
hears the answering, ageless warnings
         of the ewes.

Spring summons her
the spring of her twentieth birthday,
fervent, she cycles the lanes
on her 'iron steed'
unencumbered by petticoats
(or chaperones), speeding to the wildwood
       *the full woods overflow*
       *among the meadow's gold!*
entranced, lingering, pencilling a poem…
       *a bluebell wave has rolled,*
       *where crowded cowslips grow.*
She is an apostle of wonder
nature her book of revelation.

Collapse
fever, endless burning,
unable to eat, unable to drink,
     an ice cube on her tongue
all that she can take –
the butterfly gland betrays her
life fluttering in the balance
betwixt and between
life and death

at the point of extinction
cessation of form
like a bird winging into air
from the tip of the topmost branch.
What is death?
       *a white gate swinging on the infinite.*

Coaxed back by birdsong
by fragrance of flowers
texture of petals, voice of grass
her father's care, consoling tones
his readings from Shakespeare.

Convalescent
on her couch on the summer lawn
listening to the leaves rise and fall
an ever-coming tide

with autumn
the shock in the mirror
the fear of rejection

she will hide her eyes
conceal her throat –
always from this time on
the wide-brimmed hats
high-necked dresses
bows, tulle scarves

yet still there is solace
shelter, spiritual heightening
her temple the green world
where
      *no distortion of body*
        *frightens the birds*
they come about her, rest
on her shoulders, so still
she sits, listening, watching,

writing down the remembrance
of all she's received; immersed
in the complex life of Nature
she sees the *Soul of the World*
in the flash of underwings
plovers over ploughland.
Writing her *little book of healing*
seeking, finding again
>                    *the spring of joy.*


### Maesbrook, Meole Brace, 1902–12

Watermusic, incessant from the mill-stream.
A hammock between trees on the upper lawn
where she nestles, listening to visitants
from the *dove-grey hour* of dawn
to dusky close of day –
>            *silver-throated birds came all day long*
>            *and haunted it with ecstasies of song...*

The old Mill House, two storeys high
on a rising bank. Her window, always
open, bringing the breath of meadows,
bringing blackbirds' fluting, sedge-warblers'
prelude to dawn.

Her zest returning, she watches the ousel
dipping in the stream, the rushing weir,
her father planting saplings by the water,
walking each day his path across the fields –
and when she ventures forth at last
his arm to cling to, his reassuring glance.
Walking in Meole Brace with a downward look,
eyes hidden beneath the wide-brimmed hat,
her steps are quick, light, furtive as a small brown bird.

### Dark Weather

Christmas, 1908
veils of snow on the windows
meadows white-over,
swirling drifts cutting off Maesbrook
trees mantled, fir and pine
and all the guardians of the mill-race
sad, like the drooping boughs
her father bereft of two fine sons
a world away in other snows
claimed by Canada's call.
No puns, no bright verse to greet the season
sunk in his study, writing his last poems…
> *Draw down the blinds! – the landscape seemed so fair*
> *When all my boys and girls were playing there…*

And then within her heart a sorrow creeps
and creeps and grows into a *wild despair.*

Gone, her soul's companion,
*the wordless glance that defies fate*
protecting, encouraging, praising,
the loving presence at her sickbed,
the mind stored with beauty
the lantern in the dark.

*On that last night*, watching by his bed
she heard the tender words he whispered
*'your work is very beautiful, my sweet.'*

Grief grounds her in its charnel-grip.
Negation gnaws. Fever returns…
yet, for him she will continue. Poems out of pain –
> *The footpath that he trod each day*
> *Among the changing grass is gone…*

*These are my treasures: just a word, a look,*
*A chiming sentence from his favourite book...*

until – water sparkling in a spring – the sign
       *Life's design*
          *must yet be stitched.*

         *

Lady Day, Feast of the Annunciation, 25th March,
first day of the Spring Quarter.
An acceptance. Her story in *Country Life* –
like the first snowdrop, her first success shines:
*A Cedar Rose* by 'Lady Day' –
and soon for her
         *life's dark cedar*
         *will bear its immortal flower.*

## 4. An Apocalypse of Love

*'I have found him whom my soul loveth,*
*I held him and would not let him go.'*
           Song of Solomon

They are lovers striding the grassy heights,
exulting in their harmony of minds.
He talks of the moon's silences, Endymion,
she of the seasons she knows like a rosary
sharing her findings in hedgerow and meadow
showing him the roads *in the leaf of a nettle.*

For him she will spill
the chalice of her pride.
Have they found it? Have they found
*the golden arrow* –
a love that hurts, a love that heals?

60

### Holy Trinity, Meole Brace, 12 June 1912

*The thorn is white-over*
and she is radiant.

A large hat rimmed with flowers
dress high in the collar –
creamy muslin for country girls –
adorned only by a sash
of symbolic blue, a silk ribbon
the colour of sky, of sky reflected in water,
a holy colour, and in her hands
a bouquet of wild flowers.
Her one little bridesmaid, the gardener's daughter,
her seventy guests from the Shrewsbury poor,
the old and destitute,
herbalist, organ-grinder,
a one-eyed beggar who'd come to her door.

And from Cross Houses Workhouse
let out for the day
   all the old women enclosed in grey
   all the old men who loved a 'do'
brought by special arrangement
crowding aisle and pew
in their sad-coloured garments.

Emerging into sunshine
he looks at her, protective, amused;
she looks to him
        *as flowers to warm heaven*
        *as winter birds to a fruited tree...*
A marquee on the lawn
teacups filled and refilled
a feast for the famished
sharing her special moment.
The wedding cake's cut, brought round
twice, one old man wheezing in delight
'this time give us a piece that dunna bend.'

### Rose Cottage, and The Nills, Pontesbury, 1914–16

Down Hinton Lane
>                    *two rows of larches lean,*
>                    *and lissom, rosy pines with wild black hair*
their roof-tree Rose Cottage
>                    *in blossom-time and berry-time and snow*
and they are writing, writing
in creative flight and song
>                    *so utterly at one*
ardent, in nature's largesse
>                    *the huge folds of the hills*
>                    *the starless cwms*
Oh, Cariad!

Sunset staining the west.
The singing of soldiers
drifts from train windows
speeding south

men sucked away
>                    *gone to earth –*
and telling their deaths over
the drawn-down blinds, the wreaths,
tolling of bells, the empty village streets...

Wounded stretchered back from the Front,
broken, gassed, bandages oozing.
Red and black, the colours of death
colours of the hunt. She writes an allegory,
a country tragedy, a cry against cruelty
>                    *Hazel* and *Foxy... small, sentient...*
a cry against carnage, inhumanity,
>                    *The death-pack hunts at all hours*
pity for victims, the vulnerable, the prey...

## Spring Cottage, Lyth Hill, 1917–27

Lyth Hill. Celestial light
across the plain, gold-green,
>    *I have come to heaven*
>    *unbeknown to myself...*
The blue encircling hills
parameters of her life,
the old coppice, her Little Wood
here she contemplates each day
>    *the pointed leaves*
>  *came swiftly in green fire to meet the sun...*

Their own home, built near the wooded rim,
>  *where through black ash-buds gleams the purple hill*
two oak desks side by side,
one bedroom, a verandah.
Her large advances from publishers. London, USA.
£300 for *The House in Dormer Forest*.
His rejection slips.


## 5. Ladysmock

Lady's Smock, delicate wild flower,
palest shades of pink or lilac,
tall stems, distinct leaflets,
flowering March to June
in meadows, damp woodland verges.

Along the grassy plateau
she wanders with the neighbours' children,
pointing out, naming every bird, species
of each butterfly, bush and flower,
creating an Eden on a Shropshire hill.
A gift of names, a gift returned –
thin as a wand in her lilac dress,
fragile, smiling, a fairy godmother –

the children name her Ladysmock,
in their hands wild flowers
in their minds discovery.
Time to turn home, to their mothers and tea –
from her wicket gate she watches them go
watches them with longing, and lovingly
>  *But my baby, ah! my baby*
>  *Weepeth – weepeth*
>  *In the far loneliness of nonentity,*
>  *And holds his little spirit hands to me...*

Her Christmas list. For every child
on Lyth Hill a gift. Ladysmock's notebook
taken by young Jack Thorne from cottage
to cottage. Her instructions – ask every girl and boy,
put against their names what each one wants...

Dora Aston... gloves and stockings
the three Mold girls, cloche hats,
>           grey, green, mauve
Ena Richards... a book of Fairy Tales
John Price... a football
Evvie Price... a china cup and saucer
ages of the 3 Lewis girls?
David Mytton's size in shoes?
Laura Taylor... a piano.

The mere. Ringed by woods, waterlilies
>      *the long trembling shadows of the rushes*
her long watching, day by day
in this place of *unbreathing quiet*
creating a tapestry, the world of *Sarn*,
warp and weft of words,
>      *a core of sweetness in much bitter*
water-images of herself, her *dear acquaintance*.
But darker reflections, bells sounding deep down...

she senses
>*a breath of October in our May*

he is not content…
>*Ten thousand stars are drowned*
>*within the lake.*


## 6. Hiraeth

*London, 1921–27*

Long ago the charmed circle –
now only the Bookman Circle,
P.E.N. meetings, gatherings at Anerley
around silver-voiced de la Mare;
only the dusty city trees, foggy water
of the Thames, crumbling stucco
and destitutes at every corner…

for the consumptive boy and his family
>two weeks at the seaside

for the gassed soldier a shop with fittings
for the ragged children of Hampstead
>*a strawberry feast…*

to their cramped cottage editors come
literary men offering friendship, reviews,
but she aches for Lyth Hill, *the clear, bright grass,*
*the enchanted plain* where
>*cloud shadows pass.*

Proofs arrive by post from *The Spectator* –
and fresh from her Shropshire garden
a box of spring flowers sent by her neighbour
>*I did not think the violets came so soon*
>*Yet here are five, and all my room is sweet…*

She is a migrant bird, fleeing home
to emptiness, his icy absence.

## 5 Grove Cottages, September 1927

For Muriel Cullis... a doll and cot –
an eiderdown, a pillow.

She is stitching, stitching with shaking fingers.
Early autumn at Hampstead
the heath's red squirrels scatter
dash upwards as a man and girl
approach, hand in hand
beneath the golden leaves.

She sits alone, stitching, stitching
making gifts for the Christmas
she will not see; embroidery unfinished
like her manuscript, her medieval story
of love's treachery.

*

Then
the flower closed its petals
holding the light within,
her blackbird in the lime tree
ceased its song.

Forty-six years, so short a while
to spend in listening.

### To Henry Webb

*Died 19 August 1939 on Scafell*

Wastwater, sullen in the August sun,
scree-flanked depths, icy in the heat.
You climbed the barren heights
not fearing Scafell's awesome eminence,
strode, with a purpose, to the Pinnacle.
Another walker talked, intruded
on your thoughts, your plan.
Did you see, ironically, a reflection
of yourself in the rocks named Higher Man
and Lower Man? As you scanned
the crests and peaks, did you recall
your gentle Shropshire hills – Long Mynd,
the Wrekin, Pontesford and little Lyth –
for Mary her *home of colour and light?*
And were you haunted by her smile,
veil of dark hair and anxious eyes
at dawn, her whispered words –
*my dear, my dear* – worries spoken
and unspoken?

Love was the armour
wherein she trusted.
You knew its weakest part
yet pierced through and through
with your spear of betrayal.

Perhaps on Scafell's precipice
you faced a circled fate,
looked down Deep Ghyll
to a hidden valley
knowing foxgloves grew there, too –
more true for you than passion flowers –
bearers of death to the heart.

## Green Gravel

*(Folk Song)*

*Green gravel, green gravel*
*Your grass is so green,*
*The fairest young damsel that ever was seen,*
*I'll wash you in new milk*
*And dress you in silk,*
*And write down your name*
*With a gold pen and ink.*
*Oh Mary, oh Mary, your true love is dead.*
*He sent you a letter*
*To turn round your head.*

*Green gravel, green gravel...*

Mary Webb (1881–1927): Shropshire novelist, poet, mystic, author of *Precious Bane, Gone to Earth* and four other novels. The two greatest influences on her were her father and the Shropshire countryside of the Welsh Border, the setting and source of her work. Her love of this countryside was of an intensity and intimacy comparable with that of Emily Brontë for the Haworth moors.

Throughout this sequence details are drawn from my two biographies of Mary Webb, *The Flower of Light* (1978, reprint 1998) and *Mary Webb* (1990, reprint 1996). Additional material is from my private collection and archives, and also my editions of Mary Webb's work in *Mary Webb: Collected Prose and Poems* (1977) and *Selected Poems* (1987), and *The Spring of Joy: a Little Book of Healing* (1981 edn).

Quotations from the work of Mary Webb are in italics. The title of the sequence is from a poem by Mary Webb.

### 1. Child of Spring
She was born Mary Gladys Meredith at Leighton Lodge, 25 March 1881, to George Edward Meredith, tutor and country gentleman, and his wife Sarah Alice, formerly Scott, only child of a rich Edinburgh surgeon, Dr Walter Scott.

### 2. Her Shropshire Eden
George Edward Meredith, an Oxford M.A., ran a boarding school for boys at his home. Mary was taught by her father and attended his school until the age of ten when a governess was appointed.
*precious bane:* her father's nickname for her in childhood, quoting from Milton's *Paradise Lost*. Years later, this phrase, holding special relevance, became the title of her last completed novel.
*dear little girlie:* the term of affection used by her father.

### 3. The Bible of Pain
In Spring 1900 Mary suffered the onset of Graves' Disease, then an incurable endocrine disorder (thyrotoxicosis) resulting in protrusion of the eyes and a small goitre. This disease caused her ill-health in varying degrees for the rest of her life and contributed to her death at the age of forty-six.
*the butterfly gland:* the thyroid gland.
*the spring of joy:* at this time, recovering from severe illness, she began the series of nature essays (her first prose work) which, years later, was published by Dent (1917).

George Edward Meredith died on 5 January 1909. Mary's grief was so prolonged that she again became seriously ill with Graves' Disease.

**4. An Apocalypse of Love**
Mary married Henry B.L. Webb (1885–1939), a Cambridge graduate, teacher and writer, whom she met in Meole Brace.
*the golden arrow:* Mary adapted this legend associated with Pontesford Hill, using it symbolically, and also as the title of her first novel, written in the early years of her marriage and published in 1916 by Constable.
*gone to earth:* the title of Mary Webb's second novel, written in the year of the Somme and published in 1917 by Constable.

**5. Ladysmock**
Mary had no child of her own, although she desperately wanted one. *The mere:* this was Bomere Pool to which she would walk across the fields from Lyth Hill. Here she gathered details and inspiration for her novel *Precious Bane*. This novel was written partly at Spring Cottage and partly in Hampstead, London. It was published by Jonathan Cape in 1924 and won the *Prix Femina Vie Heureuse*.

**6. Hiraeth** (Welsh: acute longing for home)
The Webbs moved to London in 1921 when Henry Webb took a teaching post at the King Alfred School, near Hampstead. They lived in rented accommodation, keeping their Lyth Hill home, to which, sadly for Mary, Henry was increasingly unwilling to return. *her medieval story: Armour Wherein He Trusted*, her unfinished novel posthumously published in 1929.
Mary Webb died on 8 October 1927.
Henry Webb married Kathleen Wilson, his former pupil, twenty-three years younger than himself, in September 1929.

**Green Gravel**
A Shropshire folk song, quoted in *Precious Bane* and adapted here.

# ACKNOWLEDGEMENTS

Some of the poems in this collection, or versions of them, have previously appeared in the following journals and anthologies: *Ambit, Envoi, The Interpreter's House, The New Welsh Review, Poetry Wales, Poetry Nottingham International, Roundyhouse, Smoke; Blodeuwedd: An Anthology of Women's Poetry, Both Sides of the Border, A Cheshire Christmas, Lancaster Litfest Competition Anthologies 1995 and 1997, North Wales Newspapers, Poet's England Vol 20: Cheshire, Poet's England Vol 21: Derbyshire, The Poet's View: Poems for Paintings in the Walker Art Gallery, The Wilfred Owen Association Newsletter, Windfall.*

Various poems have been broadcast on BBC Radio Wales, BBC Network North-West 'Write Now', BBC Radio Merseyside, and BBC Radio Shropshire.

Sections of 'Kingdom of Sphagnum' won prizes in the Scottish International Poetry Competition and the York Open Poetry Competition, and were runner up in the Marches Prize. 'Malcolm Lowry in Paradise Street' and 'Terra Incognita' were prizewinners in the Lancaster Litfest Poetry Competition, 1995 and 1997. 'Augury' was a prizewinner in the Library of Avalon Competition 1999.

I wish to thank Dr Joan L. Daniels of English Nature, Site Manager at Fenn's,Whixall and Bettisfield Mosses National Nature Reserve, for her advice and interest in the sequence 'Kingdom of Sphagnum'; also Nigel Jones, author of *Shropshire Mosses and Meres*; and Fred Edwards, whose fine photographs of the Mosses first inspired me.

I am grateful to Mythstories Museum, Shrewsbury, for interest in my Mary Webb poems 'The Land Within' and for hosting my reading of this sequence prior to publication.

My special thanks and appreciation to Margaret Harlin and Wendy Bardsley for constant encouragement.

The title of the collection, *The Echoing Green*, is from a poem by William Blake.